Canary island cuisine

suculent and natural

EVEREST

Contents

Introduction

1 | A little bit of History

The Canary Islands owe their many highly idiosyncratic features to the unrivalled geographical position they enjoy in the Atlantic Ocean. Lying as it does in a truly privileged setting just off the southern coast of Morocco, the Canary archipelago comprises seven large islands - Lanzarote, Fuerteventura, Gran Canaria, Tenerife, Gomera, Hierro and La Palma -, along with six islets, namely Graciosa, Montaña Clara, Alegranza, Roque del Oeste, Roque del Este and Isla de los Lobos. Together, they make up the Autonomous Community of the Canary Islands.

For centuries the Islands appeared on seafarers' maps as the westernmost limit of terra firma. Subsequent to the discovery of the New World, however, they became the last port of call for ocean-going vessels that resupplied here before crossing the Atlantic. Consequently, throughout the history of the Canaries and of their native people, the Guanches, the sea has been the source of a succession of perilous episodes and invasions. Fortunately, though, the ocean waters have also brought the Islands the immense benefits and great knowledge to be derived from contact with other worlds and cultures. Furthermore, this "opening up" of the Canaries has also entailed the introduction of numerous foreign species of flora and fauna which, with the passing of time, have become adapted to such a degree that today they are considered to be native.

The origin of the Canary archipelago is to be attributed to volcanic activity, its genesis having taken place at a site in the Atlantic that Greek mythology has shrouded in legend. Indeed, it was here that Plato, in his work Critias, located the colossal island of Atlantis which, lying beyond the Pillars of Hercules, met a cataclysmic fate and sank beneath the waves. However much this may seem to belong to the realm of fable, the fact remains that the first trustworthy report of the existence of the Islands was that obtained by Plutarch from a group of fishermen from Cadiz in the year 82 B.C. Dating from the 6th century is the legend of the Irish monk Brandan, who set off on the back of a whale in search of the

The great expanses covered by banana plantations are a characteristic feature of the landscape of the Canary Islands.

Garden of Eden. The Islanders, however, mistook the sea creature for an island, which they named San Borondón. According to local tradition, San Borondón, held to be the eighth Canary Island, occasionally rises up from amidst the waters only to vanish again before any seafarers are able to discover its secrets. The Romans referred to these islands as Las Islas Afortunadas ("the Fortunate Isles") on account of the pleasant climate and the many gifts bestowed upon them by nature. Subsequent to the fall of the Roman Empire, the archipelago would be called *Kaledat* by the Arabs and became known to Europeans when the Genoese explorer Lancerotto discovered them and gave his name to the island we know today as Lanzarote. Although the ultimate conquest of the Canaries would not take place until the 15th century, the first expeditions to the archipelago were undertaken a century earlier by vessels from Majorca, Andalusia, Biscay and Portugal. The conquest was heralded in 1402 by the arrival of Normans Jean de Bethencourt and Gadifer de la Salle, who managed to discover Lanzarote but, unable to continue unaided, had to place themselves under the orders of Henry III of Castile. Bethencourt

Livestock farming is a Canary tradition that harks back to the times of the Protoguanches.

went on to subjugate the islands of Lanzarote, Fuerteventura, Hierro and La Gomera. He returned to his homeland in 1405, whereupon these minor islands came under the control of the Count of Niebla and the Pedraza family. Diego de Herrera, himself married to Inés de Pedraza, granted the right to conquer the major islands to the Catholic Monarchs. Thus, subsequent to the subjugation of Gran Canaria (1477), Alonso Fernández de Lugo set about conquering La Palma (1492) and Tenerife (1496), which completed the Spanish *conquista* of the archipelago. In what was a foretaste of the vital role to be played by the Islands on the Atlantic shipping routes,

Christopher Columbus put in at Gran Canaria in 1492 on the famous voyage that culminated in the discovery of the New World. At the time of the conquest, although the original inhabitants of the Canary Islands were of a most heterogeneous nature, they were dominated by the Guanches, a people that has been identified with Cro-Magnon man and which appeared in its purest form on Tenerife. Forming as they did an ethnical complex originating from different parts of the world, the Guanches came to the Islands in a succession of waves as from the Late Neolithic. The first to arrive were a mixed race whose forebears were North African Cro-Magnons from the Upper Palaeolithic and

5

Protoberberic Mediterraneans. The second such wave comprised troglodytic farmers whose culture is reminiscent of the peoples that inhabited Northern Africa during the Neolithic, whereas the third influx was that of by Mediterranean-Atlantic subrace, one that occupied Gran Canaria and whose last remaining vestiges, featuring stone dwellings and megalithic burials, are located at Gáldar. Further groups would arrive by sea from the eastern Mediterranean. Among the surviving artefacts belonging to the Protoguanche culture are carved stone (tabona), basalt or obsidian tools and other items such as spears, rulers' staffs and shepherds' crooks. Guanche agricultural activity centred around barley crops and a variety of wheat called yrichen, whilst their livestock farming, based on sheep, goats and pigs, also featured the use of dogs in herd management. Owing to the presence of arable land, pastures and water, the population lived in huts in small settlements or in groups of natural or man-made caves.

Worthy of particular note here are the menceyatos (regions into which the islands were divided) and the *paraderos* (the areas in which volcanic rock was worked).

Guanche mummies at the Santa Cruz Museum.

A proven relation connecting the Islands and Egypt has been established regarding the mummification of the dead, here referred to as *mirlar*. The social hierarchy of the Guanches ranged from the king or mencey right down to the peasants or achinaxcas, and also included the noblemen or *achimenceys* and the servants or *chichiciquitzos*. Social organisation was based on the patriarchal monogamous family, whilst little is known about the spiritual life of the Guanches, except for their veneration of the dead and the existence of priests and priestesses. Achaman was the supreme celestial being revered by the Islanders, who also

worshipped the sun and the stars. Guanche culture also featured certain matriarchal tendencies, however, as is witnessed by the polyandry that was rife on Lanzarote, the women fortune tellers and warriors of La Palma or the female right of succession. Political organisation on the easternmost islands took the shape of kingdoms, whereas the remainder were governed according to a tribal system. All the above factors were to greatly favour later efforts to Hispanicise the islands and to convert the native princes to Christianity. Subsequent to their conquest, the islands were divided administratively into royal dominions and seigniories. Moreover, a system of councils similar to the Castilian concejos was set up. Great prosperity soon came to the Canaries as a result of a booming overseas trade and sugar cane industry. Nevertheless, in addition to the constant threat posed by drought, the Islanders had to face the dangers of pirate incursions and the sporadic eruptions of the Timanfaya volcano, which in 1730 spewed lava over the best farmlands of Lanzarote. Fruit of the flourishing, inexorable cultural development of the Canaries were the - albeit vain - attempts to create a university at La Laguna and the creation of the Economic Society of Las Palmas (1777). After the tragic episode of the Spanish Civil War (1936-1939), the economy of the Canary Islands came to depend on three major sectors: agriculture and fishing; the trade boosted by their free-port status; and tourism. Since 1982 the Canaries have enjoyed a statute of autonomy under the Spanish constitution, one that respects the islands' administration by councils, guarantees the local taxation system and ensures that the cities of Santa Cruz on Tenerife and Las Palmas on Gran Canaria share the status of capital.

2 | Canary Island Cuisine: Ingredients and Specialities

Popular Canary Island culture boasts a highly subtle and varied cuisine that is brimming with exquisite dishes. Although certain aspects of the Islands' history have fallen into oblivion, the local culinary tradition is replete with emblematic dishes, versatile ingredients and characteristic eating habits. What we know as Canary Island cuisine is the result of contributions made over the centuries by peoples from a variety of countries such as Portugal, the Maghreb and Holland and, of course, by Spaniards from regions such as Extremadura, Galicia and Andalusia and those who returned to the Islands after making their fortunes in the New World. Canary Island cuisine features a number of truly singular ingredients and products, themselves the fruit of the highly particular local climatic and geographical conditions. Upon the conquest of the Islands, the traditional diet of the Islanders was modified by the introduction of certain culinary innovations that in time would give shape to the regional cuisine we know today. A cuisine that has nevertheless retained its immense variety of flavours and in which different names are still used from one island to another or from coastal to inland regions to refer to the same products and recipes. Contained in the pages of 20th-century Canary Island cookbooks are the

The natural wealth of the Canary Islands is reflected by the great variety of its products.

three widely varying types of cuisine found on the archipelago. First of all there is rural cookery, which, whilst not including either bread or milk, the former being a symbol of the well-to-do classes and the latter being reserved for the production of cheeses to be sold, does feature gofio, in the form of a variety of soups or stews accompanied by salted fish or typical country fare. Secondly we have the cookery characteristic of the affluent classes, in which such ingredients as meat, fish and eggs are seen to abound. Lastly, there is the so-called convent cookery, the Canary Island religious communities being renowned for their delicious confectionery, desserts and preserves.

Centuries ago, the native inland and coastal inhabitants of the Islands exchanged foodstuffs in order to bring balance to their diets. It is also known that they consumed barley and wheat, as well as the flour obtained both from the latter and from chickpeas, lupin seeds or any other cereal crop, which, duly toasted and ground, was to give rise to the popular dish called *gofio*.

Today gofio enjoys great popularity throughout the archipelago, even though the people of the so-called minor islands prefer a mixture of different cereal grains to be

"Gofio", which is prepared in many different ways, is one of the characteristic features of the Canary Islanders' diet.

used, including maize. In certain parts of La Palma, a form of gofio made with lupin seeds is eaten. Once the seeds have been immersed in salt water or steeped in spring water for a few days, they are left to dry and thereupon ground with a little salt. No sooner did the exquisite nature of maize gofio become known that the consumption of the other varieties declined drastically.

Nevertheless, gofio is still eaten in a wide variety of forms, ranging from the one prepared using sugar and eaten with a spoon from an

ice-cream style cornet to that blended with cold liquids and also including *gofio escaldado*, which is made by adding milk or stock to the flour and simmering the mixture over a low heat. Amongst the many other gofios to be enjoyed is one that is made with red wine or muscatel, sugar and an egg yolk; another that is kneaded with bananas or pork scratchings; and yet another that when ready is mixed with honey, mojo sauce, molasses, potatoes or figs. Last but not least, there is *beletén*, a gofio that is a favourite with shepherds and is made using sheep, goat or cow's milk obtained on the days subsequent to the animals' having given birth.

At a pastoral synodal council held in 1626 it was resolved that maize - a term etymologically related to the Taino Indian mahiz - should be referred to as *millo* on the Canary Islands, a word that itself derives from the Latin *millium*, which means millet. It was not long before maize or *millo* became one of the Islands' major crops and staple foods, on account of the great versatility of both its grain and cob. Maize cobs can be eaten tender once they have been toasted over the embers of a fire and either soaked in brine or, as is done in

some areas, steeped in red wine with sugar or muscatel. Alternatively, they can be boiled with a little salt and spread with butter, in which case they are called *piñas de millo sanco-chadas*. Having been brought to Spain from the New World, maize was first cultivated in Seville and later in Galicia, where it very quickly became adapted and eventually replaced millet as the local staple. It would appear that the maize plant was introduced to the Canary Islands from the said regions of the Spanish mainland. Ground maize grain is used in confectionery, in the preparation of soups and stews and is mixed into salads. Moreover, modern vending machines

produce an ever-popular form of maize, popcorn, which was formerly called *cochafisco* by the Islanders. *Macho* is the name given to boiled maize grain that is sprinkled with mojo sauce, whilst the crushed grain of maize and other cereals is referred to as *frangollo*. Lastly, finely ground maize grain is used in the production of maize bread and as an ingredient for confectionery.

The potato, which is called *patata* throughout the Peninsula, is known as *papa* in the Canary Islands. Having first arrived in Santa Cruz (Tenerife) from Peru in 1622, its cultivation was such a great success that today it ranks as one of the most traditional crops. Another similar tuber, bearing the name of *batata* (sweet potato, yam), was introduced into Spain in the same fashion, albeit this time from the Antilles, and, owing to a typing error, was confused with regular potatoes. Here in the Canaries the batata is used as an ingredient in black puddings and is served as a complement to the main dish eaten on the day of the pig slaughter or *gandinga*. Yellowish-flesh batatas are much prized and are known here either as ñame or *batata de yema*.

As well as being served as an accompaniment to other dishes, potatoes are eaten in the Canaries

Potatoes, or papas to the Islanders, enjoy a deep-rooted tradition in the regional cuisine and are prepared in a variety of ways: san-cochadas (boiled and buttered), arrugadas (wrinkled jacket) and as an accompaniment to other dishes.

as *papas sancocha-das or papas arrugadas*. Whereas the former are boiled with a touch of salt and buttered, the latter - preferably prepared using "black" Tenerife potatoes - are boiled in their jackets in salted water over a low flame and when tender are drained and left to dry over a low heat until they become wrinkled, hence their name (Sp. *arrugado*, wrinkled). *Papas arrugadas* are accompanied by two delicious sauces, *mojo picón verde* (green) and *mojo colorado* (red). The red variety is a spicy dressing that is ideal for the traditional gofio, as well as all grilled dishes (enyesques) and marinaded meats or fish. Served either straight or boiled, the green sauce is made using vegetable garden produce and features paprika instead of pepper, which makes it sweeter to the taste. It is the perfect complement for all fish dishes. Examples of the other mojo sauces to be savoured are a cheese variety called *mojo almogrote* and an almond relish called *mojo de almendras*.

Legumes

Amongst the legumes eaten by the Islanders in the past are vetches, peas, chickpeas and broad beans. In times of shortage, they even resorted to wild fodder plants.

Nowadays legumes are used mainly as the basic ingredient for a range of dishes. The popular *puchero canario*, for instance, is derived from the stew known on the Peninsula as *olla guisada*. A traditional element of Canary cuisine ever since the late 15th century, this substantial dish is made using meat and vegetables. Any leftovers from the puchero are frequently served up again for the evening meal or are used to make the Canary favourite called *tumbo*. Another substantial legume dish is that called *pote* which, originating from Galicia, includes vegetables, wild herbs, watercress and cereal grain.

Meats

Canary Island cuisine is renowned for making use of every last part of the pig, or the *cochino* as it is called here. Thus, the pig's tail or *templero* was traditionally hung from the kitchen doorway and would be dipped into the cooking pot for a few seconds to enhance the flavour of pork dishes before being put away for another day. Roast suckling pig is as popular on the Islands as it is in Castile and is known by the same name, *tostón*. Also used here, as an ingredient for certain typical dishes, is diced

fatty salt pork or *cuarterones*. Kid goat, goat and mutton also enjoy pride of place in traditional Canary cuisine, along with lamb, rabbit and veal... all of which, prepared as only the Canary Islanders know how, will delight even the most demanding of gourmets. A typical tapa to be enjoyed with the traditional rum aperitif or *pizco de ron* is that called *caracajas*, pieces of fried or roast pork liver served with lashings of spicy sauce.

Fish

The most commonly consumed fish in the Canary Islands are those to be found in the surrounding ocean. A number of small fish, such as sardines, anchovies, horse mackerel, porgies and parrot fish - some of which are sliced down the middle and sun-dried - are truly delicious fare much sought-after by locals and visitors alike. Curiously enough, the renowned horse mackerel or *chicharros* of Santa Cruz de Tenerife have even lent their name to the inhabitants of the city, who are referred to as *chicharreros*. Further examples of much-prized species that are cooked either fresh or dried are the grey mullet or *lisas*, the *sopimpa* - belonging to the family of scorpion fish - and dogfish, which are quartered to obtain strips called *tollos*. The true king amongst Canary Island fish, however, is the *vieja*, or parrot fish, a member of the sea bream family that has tasty flesh and whose popularity is reflected in many regional sayings and songs. Fish soup or *caldo de pescado* is traditionally made using grouper, although several other species caught in the area - such as the porgy, the red bream, the dentex and the *abadejo* or pollack (more commonly known as the codfish) - can also be used to add flavour to this dish. The origin of this caldo is to be found in the soups prepared by fisherman from the Islands when they were out at sea off the African coast. It boasts an unrivalled taste on account of the sheer quality and freshness of its ingredients, which are seasoned with onions, bread, pepper, stock and vinegar. So exquisitely subtle is the taste of the canned local fish roe, whether it is seasoned or not, that it has earned the nickname of "Canary caviar". As its name would suggest, the dish called *gallegada de pescado* was introduced to the Islands by Galician fishermen and varies in composition according to the daily catch.

Popular Canary Island culture boasts a highly subtle and varied cuisine that is brimming with exquisite dishes.

Seafood

The seafood on offer in the Canaries is basically that provided by the waters of the Atlantic. Its preparation, however, is seen to vary from place to place. Different species of crab such as the spider crab, as well as limpets, squid, *cabrillas* (sea bass), clams, winkles and oysters are just some of the seafood produce that features strongly in the regional cuisine and which, prepared in a variety of ways, delight both locals and visitors alike. Some

Canary seafood is also tinned in brine.
Caught on some of the islets of the archipelago, the crustacean known locally as the *santorra* is similar in appearance to the common lobster but is superior in quality.

Confectionery and Desserts

Such is the popularity and so widespread is the consumption enjoyed by some elements of the highly varied confectionery of the

Canaries that they are produced practically all over Spain. There are others, however, which on account of their ingredients and preparation exude an intrinsically Canary Island flavour that simply cannot be found elsewhere. Belonging to the former category are the custard-style *natillas*, creamed rice or *arroz con leche* and the pastries called *mantecados*, the latter being directly related to those made in Andalusia. Amongst the specialities originating strictly on the Islands are the local cheese cake or *quesadilla*, the so-called *delicias,* the *sopa de ingenio* which despite its name is an exquisite dessert, the sweet pumpkin filling called *cabello de ángel* and the bar made using almonds, sugar, toasted wheat and peanuts. *Pestiños* is the name of the honey-coated fried pastries that are produced by nuns at the Islands' convents. Typical Canary sweets are the *tirijala*, a soft lollipop made of honey and the *alfeñiques*, the little figures used to decorate all kinds of confectioner's goods.

Cheeses

Canary Island cheeses, featuring both cured and fresh varieties, are meticulously made using traditional methods from fresh goat's, sheep's and cow's-milk and have deservedly earned due recognition on international food markets. Depending on the type of livestock found in its pastures, each island boasts its own particular, highly characteristic cheese:
• Lanzarote is famed for a white, firm, thick-textured cheese boasting a strong flavour typical of those made from goat's milk.
• *Queso majorero* is made on Fuerteventura using goat's and sheep's milk and owes its spicy favour to the coating of its rind with olive oil and paprika.
• One of the Islands' finest cheeses is Flor, which is particular to Gran Canaria. Featuring a composition of three parts cow's milk to one part sheep's milk, Flor is well pressed, thus acquiring a creaminess and an aroma simply without compare.
• The outstandingly white, rindless soft cheese made on Tenerife is a blend of all three types of milk.
• The cheese typical of La Gomera, on the other hand, is a cured, spicy, full-flavoured variety based on a mixture of goat's and sheep's cheese.
• Combining all three types of milk, El Hierro cheese is slightly acidic and features a somewhat smoked flavour.

• Lastly, the island of La Palma produces a tasty cheese made from sheep's and goat's milk.

Wines, liqueurs and other nectars

Wine production on the Canaries is not sufficient to satisfy local consumer demands, even though the fine quality of the wines made on the archipelago has been common knowledge ever since the 16th century when they first became known overseas.

The dense regional red wines vary in quality according to their origin, are strong, tasty on the palate and are one of many shades of ruby red. Outstanding amongst the young reds is the fruity Del Monte from Gran Canaria, a perfect complement for all meat dishes. Its alcohol content is over 11.5°.

The best way to wash down any fried or grilled fish dishes, white meats and light meals is by savouring one of the Islands' different white wines. These can either be dry, young, fruity, or even demi-sec and low in acidity - such as Vino Diego -, in which case they are a fine accompaniment for desserts. They have an alcohol content of up to 14°.

The local rosé wines, which go

very well with any kind of food, should be served cold in order to fully bring out their splendid properties. They feature a faint pinkish colour with hues ranging from strawberry to orange. Some rosés have an alcohol content of over 10°.

The true highlight of traditional Canary wines is Malvasía, a full-bodied, sweet wine that owes its name to the Greek town from which its grapes originate. Sweet and demi-sec malvasías are used to accompany shellfish and both fried and boiled fish dishes, whereas the classic sweet variety is best served with dessert or cakes and pastries. Owing to its excellent bouquet, its exquisite taste and an alcohol content of up to 19°, Malvasía ranks as the best known of all Canary wines. Equally renowned for their excellence are the local fortified wines, such as Listán, Tea and Malvasía itself, which are enjoyed as an aperitif or with desserts. Amongst the wines considered to have medicinal properties are *Vino de la Abeja* and *Guarapo de Palma*. Whereas the former is made during the honey harvest, the latter is an alcohol-free extract taken from the sap of the palm-tree.

Lastly, there are a number of other highly popular local bever-

Many foreign markets have recognised the quality of Canary Island wine. Tacaronte Wine Museum.

ages, such as *mistela, guindilla, ponche* and *mejunje*. Regularly enjoyed by the Islanders, *mistela* varies in alcohol content according to the ingredients of its varieties. The drink called *guindilla* takes its name from the morello cherries (Sp. guinda) that appear in many popular Island recipes. The most widely known of Canary punches is an eggnog called *ponche de huevo* which combines sugar and rum with egg white and milk instead of the traditional tea and lemon.

Menjunje, a mixture of rum, lemon and honey, is a beverage with distinctly religious connotations, since it was served to clergymen as they went about visiting their parishioners. On concluding this brief but intense overview of the gastronomic landscape of the Canary Islands, we should remind the reader that such a wealth of culinary delights has to be savoured in person if it is to be fully enjoyed.

13

Starters, gofios and mojo sauces

easy

Tomato sauce (Salsa de tomate)

➤ 4 tablespoons olive oil │ 1 medium-sized onion │ chopped │ 1 tablespoon sugar │ salt │ 1 kg (2¼ lb) tomatoes │ skinned and seeded │ 6 cloves garlic │ peeled and whole

1 │ Put an earthenware dish on to heat and pour in the oil. When the oil is hot, first fry the garlic lightly and then the onion.

2 │ Skin and seed the tomatoes before placing them into the dish.

3 │ Add the sugar and salt and cook over a low heat for around 25-30 minutes, taking care that the sauce does not stick.

TIP
The natural, healthy and slightly bittersweet taste of this sauce enlivens many of the typical Canary dishes that without this substantial seasoning would lose part of their very essence and be less exquisite on the palate.

easy

Canary avocado sauce

(Salsa canaria de aguacate)

➤ 2 large avocado pears │ 1 red canary onion │ salt │ 1 egg yolk │ 1/4 l (9 fl oz) olive oil │ 1 little piece hot pepper │ lemon juice

1 │ Peel and stone the avocados and mix in a bowl with the egg yolk, the red onion and the lemon juice.

2 │ When ready, add the salt and pepper and crush the mixture.

3 │ Fold in the oil bit by bit, as if you were preparing a mayonnaise sauce.

4 │ This delicious sauce can be served either in individual bowls or, if preferred, in a sauceboat.

TIP
Owing to the particularly pleasant, buttery tropical taste lent by the avocado pears, this Canary sauce is especially recommended for all kinds of fish and seafood dishes.

15

elaborate

Roast liver tidbits
(Carajacas cumbreras)

➤ 1 kg (2¼ lb) liver of veal
pinch of medium-strength ground green pepper
1 teaspoon oregano
1 teaspoon paprika
1 bulb garlic
1 glass oil
1 glass vinegar
8 sprigs parsley
a little salt

1 | Clean the liver well, taking care to remove its skin. Cut into small pieces and place in a large glass-lined or ovenproof earthenware dish.

2 | Using a pestle and mortar, crush the peeled garlic together with the pepper, parsley and salt. Add the vinegar, oil, oregano and paprika. Put the mixture to one side.

3 | Pour part of the seasoning over the pieces of liver in the earthenware dish. Mix evenly by stirring slowly with a wooden spoon.

4 | Leave to marinate overnight. The following day, roast the liver pieces on a low heat.

5 | While the liver pieces are being roasted to taste, grilled or griddled, sprinkle them with some of the reserved seasoning. When done, place them back in the earthenware dish.

6 | Serve onto individual plates. Warm up the rest of the seasoning in a frying pan and sprinkle over the liver. Accompany with boiled and buttered or wrinkled jacket potatoes (papas sancochadas or papas arrugadas).

TIP Since this exquisite roasted snack is best enjoyed with an alcoholic beverage, it is popular as an appetizer washed down with a drop of Canary rum.

OBSERVATION Although the truly "genuine" caracajas are roast or fried tapas made using pork liver - the pig or cochino is known to have existed on the Islands even before the arrival of cattle in around 1500 -, the ones described in this recipe are a tasty version featuring liver of veal.

easy

Beletén gofio
(Beletén de vaca)

➤ 1 l (35 fl oz) milk, obtained first day after birth of calf
salt to taste
1/2 l (17 fl oz) water
sugar

1 | Put the water on to boil with the milk in a pan. Turn down the heat and simmer as soon as the first lumps begin to appear.

2 | Whilst the mixture is simmering, slowly stir with a wooden spoon until it diminishes a little in volume.

3 | When ready, let the mixture cool and pour it out into a serving dish. Accompany with gofio and sugar laid out in separate bowls.

NOTE In the Canary Islands, beletén is the name given to goat, cow or sheep's milk obtained on the days just after the animal has given birth.

Photograph: **Roast liver tidbits** ➤

easy

Green mojo sauce with coriander
(Mojo verde con cilantro)

➤ 12 bunches coriander
1/2 small cup oil
1 small cup vinegar
6 cloves garlic
3 tablespoons stock, preferably potato
salt

1 | Peel the garlic and pound with a pestle and mortar together with the salt and coriander.

2 | Pour the oil over the crushed garlic and coriander and stir well. Immediately add the vinegar and the stock until a smooth, compact mass is obtained.

3 | Placed in a separate sauceboat, green mojo sauce with coriander is served with fried fish dishes or buttered boiled potatoes.

NOTE

Canary mojo sauces enjoy great popularity both in their own right and as part of certain emblematic local dishes that in turn constitute the veritable heritage of Canary culinary culture. The sauce described here, which originates from the island of El Hierro, although not as hot as its red counterpart, still displays a wealth of aromas and flavours all of its own.

easy

Boilded mojo sauce (Mojo hervido)

➤ 1 pimienta picantona seca
6 dientes de ajo
1 tacita de aceite
4 ramitas de perejil
1 tacita de vinagre
1 ct de pimentón
la miga de un panecillo
1 hoja de laurel
1 tacita de agua
2 ramitas de tomillo

1 | To make the taste of the pepper a little less hot, halve and seed it and leave it to soak for 20 minutes in hot water. Drain off the water and remove the veins from the inside of the pepper, scraping it a little with a knife.

2 | Pour the vinegar into a separate bowl to soak the crumb taken from the bread roll.

3 | Clean the pepper, peel the garlic and place in a mortar along with the parsley sprigs and the vinegar-soaked breadcrumb. Mix well with the pestle.

4 | Heat the oil in a frying pan and add the mixture. Fry with the paprika, the bay leaf and the thyme.

5 | Add the water and some vinegar to the fried mixture, leaving it to simmer for a few moments until ready to be eaten.

TIP

When combined with the delicate, exquisite taste of fish, this mild, subtle sauce helps to create dishes that are simply overflowing with flavour.

Photograph: **Green mojo sauce with coriander**

refined

Fried moray
(Morena frita)

➤ 1 moray weighing 1 kg
(2¼ lb)
4 clove garlic
1/2 cup oil | salt

1 | Remove the fish's head, gut and clean thoroughly. Cut the fish lengthwise, taking care that the two halves remain joined together.

2 | Leave in salt for 30 minutes. Slice widthwise, once again taking care that the pieces remain joined together. Cover in a fine-woven cloth and hang up in the open air.

3 | Once the fish has aired, cut off the individual slices one by one with a knife and fry in a pan with the cloves of garlic, which have previously been peeled and cut into halves.

4 | Once golden brown, the moray must be left on the heat for a while until its bones have softened.

5 | Serve the fish accompanied with either of the typical Canary sauces, mojo verde or mojo colorado and, naturally, with potatoes, either papas arrugadas or papas sancochadas.

OBSERVATION

The basic difference between the Canary sauces called "mojo verde" and "mojo colorado" is that the former, a green sauce, is recommended for seasoning fish, either boiled or when raw, whereas the latter, a red sauce which has also gone under the names of "bravo", "quemón" and "picón", is characterised by its strong, hot taste.

easy

Toasted cereal mash with horse mackerel
(Gofio escaldado al estilo de los bordones)

➤ 5 tablespoons gofio
(toasted cereal flour)
200 g (7 oz) horse mackerel
1 semi-hard cheese
3 shoots of mint
1½ l (52 fl oz) potato stock
3 tomatoes, skinned, seeded and mashed
1 green pepper, cored, seeded and sliced into fine rings
1 medium-sized Canary onion, finely chopped

1 | Put an earthenware dish on to heat and pour in the potato stock. Add the onion, tomatoes and mint and simmer for a few minutes.

2 | Add salt to taste and, whilst stirring, slowly fold in the toasted flour until a smooth, uniform mass is obtained.

3 | Finally, add the horse mackerel and leave them to cook for a few seconds. Serve at the table from the same dish used for cooking and accompany with the cheese on a separate plate, each guest helping himself as required.

NOTE

As an ingredient, the term gofio refers to the flour obtained from certain cereals, such as wheat, barley or lupin. Whereas the inhabitants of Tenerife prefer to prepare this dish using wheatmeal, those of Gran Canaria replaced all other cereals with maize once they had learnt of its true potential. With the exception of La Palma, where lupin flour is the chosen variety, the rest of the Islands favour gofio made with either a "mixture" of flours or with maize.

Photograph: **Toasted cereal** ➤

elaborate

Hot red mojo sauce

(Mojo picón -bravo o colorado-)

➤ 1 dry red pepper plant, with its fruit

1/2 teaspoon cumin

1 cup oil

1 cup boiled water, left to cool

1 bulb garlic

1 level tablespoon paprika

2 small cups vinegar

salt

1 | Pound the cumin with a pestle and mortar. Open, seed and clean the peppers. Soak them in hot water for 20 minutes.

2 | After soaking, scrape the inside of the peppers, clean and core them. When clean, mix the peppers with the cumin, the peeled garlic and the salt.

3 | Immediately add the paprika and continue pounding. Stir everything in well with the pestle and pour in the oil. Stir well again and when the mixture becomes a smooth paste, add the vinegar and water, continuing to stir until everything is well mixed in.

4 | Serve the mojo picón sauce in individual earthenware dishes. A typical Canary Island seasoning, it is accompanied by wrinkled jacket or buttered boiled potatoes (papas arrugadas or papas sancochadas), which are dipped into it as they are eaten. Equally good for dunking in this sauce are pieces of bread and gofio.

NOTE Enjoying as it does widespread popularity, deep-rooted tradition and considerable prestige, this sauce reigns supreme amongst the Canary mojo sauces. Quite unlike any of the soups or dishes known on mainland Spain, mojo is a sauce made with cured raw ingredients that are steeped in and mixed with vinegar and water.

TIP Should you prefer a spicier mojo sauce, do not seed the peppers or add any water on pounding them.

easy

Milk and maize flour mash

(Escaldón de gofio y leche)

➤ 4 tablespoons toasted maize flour | 2 table-spoons sugar | 1/2 l (17 fl oz) milk | 1/4 lemon rind

1/4 cinnamon stick

1 | Pour the milk into a pan, place over a flame and bring to the boil.

2 | When the milk begins to boil, add the toasted maize flour, cinnamon, sugar and lemon.

3 | Stir the resulting gofio slowly, not stopping until the mixture comes to the boil again and thickens.

4 | Leave the milk and maize flour mash to cool. Serve up on individual plates and sweeten to taste using sugar taken from a separate sugar bowl.

NOTE "Escaldón" is a typical Canary Island dish that features many different varieties and whose basic ingredients are: toasted maize flour or gofio, garlic, saffron, pork back fat, mint and green pepper.

easy

Gofio loaf
(Pella de gofio)

➤ 200 g (7 oz) toasted maize flour
1 tablespoon olive oil
1 tablespoon sugar
1 glass water
salt

1 | Put the toasted maize flour into a mixing bowl. Dissolve the salt and sugar in water in a separate bowl.

2 | Pour the oil into the mixing bowl and add the sugar and salt solution.

3 | Knead the mixture by hand, giving the dough a round shape at either end so that it looks like a Spanish loaf of bread.

4 | Place the "loaf" (or "pella" to the Islanders) on the table. Guests serve themselves by breaking off a portion with their hands.

5 | The gofio is then worked into shape with the fist and accompanied with salted fish (sancocho) or olives.

TIP Another way of enjoying this form of gofio is to dip it as it is into a delicious Canary mojo picón sauce.

OBSERVATION Should any guest suffer from diabetes, the sugar can be replaced by salt. Another somewhat less common practice is to add a dash of mature rum.

easy

Cereal flour mash with potatoes and yams
(Gofio amasado con papas y batatas)

➤ 1 potato taken from soup or stew
1 yam (or sweet potato) of equal weight, or just a piece
3 tablespoons toasted maize flour

1 | Mash the potato and yam in a china bowl. Very slowly add the toasted maize flour and work into a fine, smooth mass.

2 | If however your guests should prefer their gofio to have a thicker consistency, simply add a larger quantity of toasted maize flour and mix thoroughly, taking care that all the ingredients bind well.

3 | Once the gofio is ready, serve in individual bowls.

TIP If you wish to save on time and effort, the toasted maize flour mash can be eaten as it was in times gone by, that is, with each guest taking his food directly from a common dish or bowl.

NOTE Potatoes were first brought to the Canary Islands from Peru and before very long were grown all over the archipelago. Whereas the Islanders have always referred to them as "papas", on the Spanish mainland, however, they were to become known as "patatas". For its part, the sweet potato, which originated in the Antilles and locally goes under the name of "batata", is used in the Canaries to accompany trout dishes or as an ingredient for sweet black puddings or morcillas. The yellow-fleshed variety, or yam, is known locally as "ñame" or "batata de yema".

Photograph: **Gofio loaf** ➤

elaborate
Snails in spicy sauce
(Chuchangos en salsa)

➤ 2 kg (4¹/² lb) snails or chuchangos | sachet of cumin | 2 sprigs fennel | 200 g (7 oz) cereal flour or gofio (toasted cornmeal)
1 bulb garlic | 1 piece orange peel | 1 level teaspoon cooking salt
1/2 tablespoon paprika
1/2 green pepper | 1 sprig thyme | 1 bay leaf
1 tablespoon oregano | 1/2 small cup of oil | a little vinegar

1 | Before cooking, the chuchangos or snails must be purged, that is, sand and slime have to be removed from their insides. To do this, wash the snails repeatedly under the tap with abundant cold water. Place in a suitable cooking dish, sprinkle with the toasted cornmeal (gofio) and the fennel and leave overnight covered with a fine gauze.

2 | After the snails have been purged, wash them thoroughly several times. When clean, return them to the dish, having filled the latter beforehand with equal parts of water and vinegar. Place on the heat and bring to the boil, removing any froth that forms on boiling with a spoon or ladle.

3 | Meanwhile, mix and crush the rest of the ingredients in a mortar, except for the bay leaf, the thyme and the oregano, which are set aside for use later.

4 | Stir the snails well. Whilst continuing to stir, add the oil and half a small wineglass of vinegar. Add the crushed mixture to the dish and cook for an hour.

5 | An hour later add the ingredients that were previously set aside. When the snails are tender, remove from the heat and eat as they are or serve with papas sancochadas (buttered boiled potatoes).

easy
Spicy potato and flour mash
(Escacho palmero)

➤ 2 cloves garlic | 1/2 kg (1 lb) potatoes | a few cumin seeds | 1 dried hot pepper
300 g (11 oz) hard cheese
toasted flour for the dough
1/2 small cup vinegar

1/2 small cup olive oil
a few tablespoonfuls stock from the boiled potatoes
a little salt

1 | Halve and seed the pepper and soak in hot water. The longer the pepper is left to soak, the milder its characteristic hot taste will become. Before placing the pepper in the mortar with the cumin seeds, the peeled garlic and the salt, remove its veins and scrape its inside with a knife.

2 | Using a pestle, crush the above ingredients into a smooth paste, mixing well and adding the oil and vinegar.

3 | Peel the potatoes and boil in salted water until tender. Salt to taste. Mash the potatoes by hand and place in a separate bowl.

4 | Pour the sauce previously prepared in the mortar over the potatoes, together with a few tablespoons of the stock left over from boiling the potatoes. Mix well.

5 | Slowly sprinkle the toasted flour over the potatoes and finally add the cheese, finely chopped, whilst stirring the mixture.

6 | Serve the resulting paste on an oblong glass platter. Cut into individual portions and enjoy as an accompaniment to stews.

Photograph: **Snails in spicy sauce** ➤

Soups, pulses and stews

elaborate
Celery stew (Potaje de colinos)

➤ 300 g (11 oz) pinto beans, if possible buttery | 4 salted pork ribs | 1 kg 2¼ lb) medium-sized potatoes | 300 g (11 oz) marrow | 5 medium-sized celery leafstalks | 2 medium-sized carrots | 4 l (140 pulg.) water | 3 cloves garlic | 250 g (9 oz) yams | 2 maize cobs | 1 tomato | 1 small onion | salt | 3 medium-sized courgettes | half red pepper, fresh

1 | Leave the beans and the pork ribs to soak overnight in separate containers. Wash the celery leafstalks and cut into medium-sized pieces.

2 | Put the water on to boil in a pot and add the beans, the pork ribs and the maize cobs. Leave to cook for a while.

3 | When the beans are cooked, chop up the po-tatoes, yams, carrots, marrow, tomato, onion and red pepper and add to the pot, along with the halved courgettes, the crushed garlic and the oil.

4 | Prick the potatoes with a fork and, if they are tender, remove the pot from the heat and leave to stand for a few moments. The stew is usually accompanied by gofio and soft cheese.

elaborate
Lentil stew (Potaje de lentejas)

➤ 1/2 kg (1 lb) lentils | salt | 300 g (11 oz) marrow | 2 clean courgettes or buangos | 4 whole maize cobs | 400 g (14 oz) chopped yam | 1 cup oil | 1/2 kg (1 lb) potatoes, peeled | 1 onion | 4 cloves garlic, peeled and chopped | 1 tomato, skinned, seeded and chopped | 1 teaspoon paprika | half sachet saffron

1 | Select the lentils carefully, rinse them and leave to soak for approximately 2 h. Wash the lentils again before putting them on to boil with the maize cobs in a cooking pot containing 4¹ᐟ² l (157 fl oz) of water.

2 | When the lentils are halfway to being done, whilst keeping them on the boil, add the halved courgettes (or buangos), the yams, the marrow and the potatoes.

3 | Meanwhile heat the oil and lightly fry the onion, the garlic, the tomatoes and the paprika, stirring now and again. When ready, pour the fried mixture over the stew, adding the saffron at the same time. Salt to taste and simmer until the potatoes are tender.

4 | When the stew is done, take it off the heat and leave to stand for 10 to 12 minutes. Serve the lentils from a soup tureen and eat whilst they are still hot.

elaborate

Fish soup

(Caldo de pescado)

- ➤ 1 x 2 kg (4½ lb) pollack
  2 kg (4½ lb) potatoes
  1 onion
  3 cloves garlic
  cooking salt
  1 small cup olive oil
  2 large tomatoes, skinned, seeded and chopped
  1 tablespoon crushed cumin seeds
  1 tablespoon paprika
  5 l (175 fl oz) water
  4 sprigs parsley
  1 ripe pepper
  mint shoots
  3 hard bread rolls, sliced
  1 sachet saffron stigmas
  4 sprigs coriander

1 | Remove the scales, gut and gills of the fish. Cut into thick slices, wash, sprinkle with cooking salt and put to one side.

2 | Peel and wash the potatoes. Put them on to boil in a pot, covering them with water and adding a touch of salt.

3 | Heat a little oil in a frying pan and fry half of the pepper

(cut into pieces) together with the peeled and chopped onions and garlic. When done, pour into the pot containing the potatoes and, after boiling for 15 minutes, add the fish, a little bunch of parsley, the coriander, the crushed saffron and part of the mint. Check that the seasoning is just right and continue boiling until the fish is done.

4 | In a small earthenware dish, set aside the butter, the toasted flour and the remainder of the mint. Adding a few previously reserved potatoes, stir uninterruptedly with a wooden spoon until a smooth, thick mash is formed.

5 | Just before the fish soup has finished cooking, pour a little stock over the slices of bread.

6 | When the soup is done, serve everything immediately, accompanied with a green mojo sauce in a separate sauceboat and a bowl of Canary salad.

TIP If you like spicy foods, add a little green hot pepper to the potato to be mashed.

easy

Chikpea and meat stew with bread (Tumbo de puchero)

- ➤ 3 tablespoons olive oil
  3 slices bread
  3 cloves garlic, peeled

1 | Put the leftovers from a puchero or chickpea and meat stew through a coarse sieve or colander. Heat up the contents of the sieve on the griddle.

2 | Remove any bones from the more substantial pieces caught in the sieve and set the latter aside.

3 | Put a frying pan on to heat and pour in the oil. Fry the garlic until golden brown and then add the meat and the chickpeas. Cook until golden brown. Set aside to serve hot.

4 | Place 3 slices of bread on each individual plate. Pour a ladleful of very hot stock (from the stew) over the bread and leave until it is all soaked up. Eat first of all the slices of bread prepared as above, followed by the fried mixture previously set aside.

easy

Potato soup

(Caldo de papas)

- ➤ 1¹/₂ kg (3¹/₄ lb) new potatoes
  6 cloves garlic | salt
  1/2 sachet cumin seeds
  1 teaspoon paprika
  1 ripe tomato
  1/2 bunch coriander
  3 l (105 fl oz) water
  6 sprigs parsley
  1 medium-sized onion
  1 egg per person (6 in total) | 1/2 cup olive oil

1 | Pour the water into a pot and put it on to boil. Peel the potatoes, halving the larger ones, and add to the water, along with the onion, once peeled and halved, and the unskinned tomato, seeded and halved.

2 | Place the garlic, the parsley, the cumin seeds, the salt, the paprika and the oil in a mortar. Crush well with the pestle, stir and add to the pot.

3 | When the potatoes are almost done, add the bunch of coriander and the saffron. When the potatoes have gone soft, add the eggs one by one before removing the pot from the heat.

4 | Leave to stand for just a few moments. Place on the table and serve steaming hot.

TIP Use more potatoes in the preparation of this soup if some are to be reserved to make gofio, either as an accompaniment to other dishes or as a meal in itself.

elaborate

Rocket stew

(Potaje de jaramagos)

- ➤ 1 kg (2¹/₄ lb) jaramagos (rocket)
  100 g (4 oz) streaky bacon
  150 g (5 oz) potatoes
  250 g (9 oz) pinto beans
  250 g (9 oz) fresh pork meat
  100 g (4 oz) white sweet potato
  1/2 green pepper
  4 cloves garlic
  150 g (5 oz) yellow sweet potato
  1/2 teaspoon paprika
  1/2 small cup oil | salt
  1/2 sachet cumin seeds

1 | Leave the beans to soak overnight. Wash the rocket under the tap in abundant cold water, separating the stems from the leaves.

2 | Put the beans, the pork meat and the cleaned streaky bacon on to boil in a pot. When half cooked, add the rocket stems, previously cut into pieces, along with the sweet potatoes and potatoes, all chopped, and the paprika.

3 | Crush the garlic and the cumin seeds, add the pepper and pour into the cooking pot together with the oil.

4 | Before adding the rocket leaves to the pot, boil them in water to neutralise their bitter taste. Drain.

5 | Try the potatoes and if they are soft, remove them from the heat and leave to stand. This dish is accompanied by toasted flour or gofio, which is mixed on a separate plate with stock from the stew, some potatoes and a bit of sweet potato.

TIP Round off this dish accompanying it with a toasted maize flour "loaf" (pella de gofio) or alternatively with one of the many Canary Island salads.

elaborate

Vegetable stew
(Potaje de verduras)

➤ 250 g (9 oz) beans, tender
4 pork ribs | salt
4 l (140 fl oz) water |
4 cloves garlic
4 tender maize cobs
1/2 kg (1 lb) cabbage
1 large tomato
1 medium-sized onion
1/2 kg (1 lb) yams
1 kg (2¼ lb) medium-sized potatoes
1/2 kg (1 lb) marrow
1/2 kg (1 lb) courgettes
1/2 kg (1 lb) green beans
3 sprigs parsley
3 sprigs coriander
pinch of cumin seeds

1 | Put the 4 litres of water on to boil in a pot. Add all the green vegetables, once they have been washed and cut into pieces.

2 | Wash and halve the maize cobs. With a knife, pierce the onion in the middle. Skin and seed the tomato.

3 | One after the other, add the beans, the 4 pork ribs, the cob pieces, the whole onion and the tomato.

4 | Whilst the mixture is cooking, crush the parsley sprigs, the cumin seeds and the coriander using a pestle and mortar.

5 | After the soup has been cooking for 15 minutes, add the yams, the halved potatoes and the crushed seasoning.

6 | Remove the potatoes from the heat as soon as they become tender and leave to stand for about 12 minutes. Place the soup on the table in a tureen and serve using a ladle.

elaborate

Watercress
stew (Potaje de berros)

➤ 1/2 kg (1 lb) watercress |
2 cobs
100 g (4 oz) streaky bacon
200 g (7 oz) beans, tender
4 pork ribs, fresh
200 g (7 oz) yellow sweet potatoes
150 g (5 oz) yams
1 kg potatoes
some cumin seeds | 4 l (140 fl oz) water
pinch of paprika
4 cloves garlic | 1 onion
1/2 small cup oil | salt

1 | Clean the watercress well, removing the thickest stems. Wash and cut into pieces.

2 | Wash the pork ribs if they are fresh; if using salted ribs, wash in hot water and leave to soak for a few hours.

3 | Pour the water into a pot and add the ribs, bacon, beans, yam and sliced cobs. When these are halfway to being cooked, also add the watercress, cumin seeds, finely chopped sweet potatoes, paprika and oil. Salt to taste, stir well and simmer for 1 hour.

4 | Later, prick the potatoes with a fork. If they are soft, leave the stew to stand for 15 minutes and then serve from a tureen accompanied by gofio.

TIP

The gofio or toasted flour is placed on the table in a separate bowl so that it can be mixed to taste with a few tablespoons of stock from the stew. Should this be too much trouble, some gofio and soft cheese may be placed on the edge of each individual plate.

Photograph: **Vegetable stew** ➤

elaborate

Rancho canario

➤ 300 g (11 oz) Canary chickpeas

150 g (5 oz) chorizo

125 g (4¹⁄² oz) chicken meat

100 g (4 oz) streaky bacon

125 g (4¹⁄² oz) pork spare rib

4 cloves garlic | 1 onion

2 tomatoes, seeded

1 small cup olive oil

4 sprigs parsley, chopped

1 sachet saffron

5 l (175 fl oz) water

1 kg (2¹⁄⁴ lb) potatoes, peeled

100 g (4 oz) thick vermicelli

1/2 teaspoon cumin seeds, crushed by hand

1/2 small cup Canary wine

1 tablespoon paprika | salt

1 | Leave the chickpeas to soak overnight. Drain and wash them before preparing the dish.

2 | Pour all the water into a pot and put on to boil. When hot, add the chickpeas along with the streaky bacon, the meat, the chorizo and the salt.

3 | Using a skimmer, take the meat out of the pot when tender. Place in a bowl on one side, shred and remove any bones. Return the meat to the pot.

4 | Meanwhile, heat the olive oil in a pan and fry the onion, garlic, tomatoes, paprika, cumin seeds and parsley. Add wine and pour the mixture into the pot, together with the potatoes (cut into pieces) and the saffron.

5 | When the potatoes are almost done, add the vermicelli and leave to boil for a few moments. When ready, remove the pot from the heat and leave to stand for 15 minutes before eating.

for guests

Canary red grouper and potato stew

(Sancocho canario)

➤ 2 kg (4¹⁄² lb) salted red grouper

2 kg (4¹⁄² lb) regular-sized potatoes, whole

1/2 kg (1 lb) toasted cereal flour

1/2 kg (1 lb) yams or yellow sweet potatoes, cut into pieces

1/4 l (9 fl oz) hot mojo sauce

5 l (175 fl oz) water | salt

1 | Leave the fish to soak overnight, taking care to replace the water 2 or 3 times during the 12-hour soaking process.

2 | In the morning, remove the scales from the fish, cleaning it thoroughly. Break into pieces of about 200 g (7 oz). Set aside so that the fish can drain a little.

3 | Put a pot on to boil with water and salt. First of all add the sweet potatoes, followed by the potatoes. Leave to cook for about 10 to 12 min, add the fish and remove froth with a ladle.

4 | When the potatoes are done, drain off the surplus water from the cooking pot and return to the heat to allow the remaining water to fully evaporate.

5 | Sancocho canario is served up on a tray, the fish laid out in the middle, flanked on one side by the sweet potatoes and on the other by the potatoes. To lend the dish greater personality and flavour, accompany with a sauce boat containing mojo picón (hot mojo sauce).

TIP Round off this dish accompanying it with a toasted maize flour "loaf" (pella de gofio) or alternatively with one of the many Canary Island salads.

Photograph: **Canary red grouper and potato stew** ➤

Fish and shellfish

easy

Squid fried in batter
(Calamares rebozados)

➤ 1 kg (2¼ lb) squid | 2 eggs | 1 small bottle beer | 1/4 kg (9 oz) flour | 2 cloves garlic | 1 cup olive oil | a little lemon juice

1 | Remove the outer fleshy part of the squid and wash under the tap in abundant cold water. Take out the insides, remove the hard parts and wash well. Cut the flesh of the squid into rings and drain these on a tray.

2 | Meanwhile, crack the eggs into a bowl, pour in the beer and beat well. Whilst still beating, fold the flour in slowly until a fine batter is obtained. Add the chopped garlic and parsley.

3 | Once dry, place the squid rings in the batter and leave to soak for about 15 minutes. Heat the oil in a pan until hot and fry the squid rings until golden brown.

4 | On removing successive batches of squid rings from the pan, place on sheets of kitchen paper. When the paper has absorbed all the oil, spread the rings out on a serving platter.

5 | Sprinkle the squid rings with lemon juice whilst still hot and serve.

easy

Fresh roe in batter
(Huevas de pescado fresco rebozadas)

➤ 1/2 kg (1 lb) fresh roe | 4 sprigs parsley, chopped | 2 tablespoons flour | 4 cloves garlic, chopped | 1/2 lemon | 1/2 teaspoon oregano | oil for frying | 2 eggs | water | salt

1 | Put the roe on to boil in the water with salt and lemon. Once cooked, drain and wait until it is cool.

2 | Cut the roe into slices, coat in flour and dip into the previously beaten mixture of eggs, garlic and parsley.

3 | Heat plenty of oil in a pan and fry the roe slices. When done, serve accompanied by wrinkled jacket potatoes and one of the fine Canary Island mojo sauces.

NOTE

Commonly known as "Canary caviar", the local fish roe - either dried or fresh - is enjoyed in a variety of ways, such as boiled, dried or seasoned. It ranks as one of the Canary Islanders' favourite foods.

39

easy

Dogfish in sauce

(Tollos en salsa)

➤ 1 kg (2¼ lb) dogfish, in strips | 1 cup olive oil
6 sprigs parsley | salt
1/2 kg (1 lb) tomatoes
1 medium-sized pepper
6 cloves garlic | cumin seeds
1/2 kg (1 lb) onions
1 teaspoon paprika
1 sprig thyme
1 bay leaf | 1 glass wine
dry Malvasía wine

1 | Cut the dogfish into strips and leave to soak overnight, taking care to change the water 2 or 3 times.

2 | Drain and wash the fish well, braise and place on one side in an ovenproof dish.

3 | Peel the onions and skin the tomatoes. Cut into pieces. Chop up the pepper and fry all together in hot oil until golden brown.

4 | Crush the cumin seeds, the paprika, the bay leaf and the garlic in a mortar, adding the salt and the wine to the mixture. Pour into the saucepan

and fry together with the dogfish strips.

5 | Remove from the heat when the fish is tender (check this by prodding with a fork).

TIP
Should the sauce in the frying pan dry up, add a little hot water.

OBSERVATION
This typical Canary Island dish is made with "tollos", which is the name given to the strips obtained by cutting up dogfish. The flesh of this predatory species is very tasty and is sold by weight in bundles.

refinate

Clams in Canary sauce

(Almejas en salsa canaria)

➤ 1 kg (2¼ lb) fresh clams
5 cloves garlic
2 tablespoons milk
1 large onion
ground black pepper
1/2 small cup salt for soaking | pinch of salt

1 bay leaf
1 tablespoon almonds, peeled and ground
1 small cup oil | 2 stigmas saffron | 6 sprigs parsley | some bread

1 | If you live in a coastal area and can easily obtain sea water, wash the clams in the latter. If not, wash them under the tap in abundant cold water.

2 | Once clean, place the clams in a bowl and cover with slightly salted water. Leave to soak for 1 hour. Wash again and drain well.

3 | Place the finely chopped, peeled onion into an earthenware dish, add the oil and bay leaf and put on the heat.

4 | When the onion becomes transparent, add the clams, the garlic (which has previously been peeled and crushed), the finely-chopped parsley and the salt. Stir the mixture and lower the heat.

5 | In a separate bowl, mix the ground almonds with the bread and milk. Pour over the clams, season with the pepper and remove from the heat 2 minutes later.

6 | Serve the clams in individual earthenware dishes. Sprinkle with their own sauce.

easy

Horse mackered in pickling brine
(Chicharros en escabeche)

➤ 1 kg (2¼ lb) medium-sized horse mackerel
olive oil for frying
4 cloves garlic
1 cup flour
2 carrots | 1 leek
1 onion | 1 bay leaf
1 glass vinegar
3 sprigs thyme | salt
1 glass white wine
3 grains black pepper
1/2 l (17 fl oz) water

1 | Clean the fish and then sprinkle with salt and flour. Heat the oil in a pan and when hot add the horse mackerel. Fry.

2 | Chop the leeks, the garlic, the onions and the carrots very finely and fry lightly in a separate pan. Add, one after the other, the bay leaf, the pepper, the vinegar, the thyme, the white wine and the water. Leave to stand for around 15 minutes.

3 | Pour this pickling brine mixture over the horse mackerel and bring to the boil for a few moments, and this delicious dish is ready to be enjoyed.

NOTE

So abundant is the horse mackerel in the ocean waters surrounding the city of Santa Cruz de Tenerife that the inhabitants of the latter are commonly known as "Chicharreros" (Sp. chicharro, horse mackerel). Referred to as "jurel" in other parts of Spain, this fish bears the scientific name of Trachurus trachurus.

elaborate

Fresh tuna in thick spicy sauce
(Atún fresco embarrado)

➤ 1 kg (2¼ lb) tuna | oil
2 cloves garlic, peeled
1/4 l vinegar | salt
Ingredients for the sauce:
1/2 tablespoon paprika
1/2 tablespoon cumin seeds
1 bulb garlic, peeled
1 cup vinegar
1 cup oil
1 dry red pepper
1/4 small cup water
3 sprigs parsley | salt

1 | Skin and fillet the tuna fish. Wash the fillets well and leave to soak in slightly salted water for 2 hours. Drain and place in vinegar for 15 minutes.

2 | Heat the oil in a pan, halve the two cloves of garlic and fry until golden brown. Fry the tuna fillets in the same oil. As soon as successive batches of fillets are done, reserve in a separate pan.

3 | To make the sauce, first cut open, core and seed the pepper and soak in hot water. 20 minutes later, take the pepper out and clean.

4 | Crush the pepper and the cumin seeds in a mortar. Add the parsley, peeled garlic and salt. Once the mixture has bound well, place in the frying pan, add the paprika and stir.

5 | Add the oil to the mixture, stir, and fold in the vinegar and water. Finally, pour the contents into a cooking dish.

6 | Put the dish with all the contents on to the heat. When it comes to the boil, spread the sauce over the tuna and accompany with buttered boiled or wrinkled jacket potatoes.

for guests

Chopped fish platter
(Salpicón de pescado)

➤ 1¹ᐟ² kg (3¹ᐟ⁴ lb) corbina (white sea bass) or red grouper | 1/2 small green pepper | 1/2 small red pepper | 6 sprigs parsley | 2 onions | 2 sprigs coriander | 4 tomatoes | 2 hard-boiled eggs | 2 tablespoons vinegar | 4 cloves garlic | salt | 1/2 small cup oil

1 | Remove the scales from the fish and wash it well under the tap with abundant water. Place into a pan with sufficient water and cook on a medium heat for 10 to 12 minutes. Take off of the heat and drain.

2 | When the fish has cooled, remove the skin and the bones. Cut into slices and arrange on a platter.

3 | Peel the onions and chop up along with the washed and seeded tomatoes and peppers. Mix together. Set aside. On a separate board, finely chop the parsley, the coriander and the garlic.

4 | Once they have been hard-boiled, cut the eggs into pieces and mix evenly into the fish.

5 | Beat the vinegar, oil and salt and add to the reserved mixture of onions, tomatoes and peppers.

6 | Finally, stir all the ingredients in well using the appropriate kitchen utensils.

TIP This chopped fish in sauce or "salpicón de pescado" is even more attractive if presented in an oblong glass serving dish decorated on top by sliced olives and pieces of hard-boiled egg.

easy

Parrotfish and potato stew
(Vieja sancochada)

➤ 1 x 1 kg (2¹ᐟ⁴ lb) fresh parrotfish | 1/2 kg (1 lb) potatoes
2 l (70 fl oz) water | salt
3 sprigs coriander |
3 sprigs parsley
1 medium-sized onion
1 medium-sized tomato

1 | Gut the fish and remove its gills. Place on a long tray, without yet removing the scales, and sprinkle its inside with salt.

2 | Pour the water into a pot and add the halved, seeded, but unskinned tomato, the peeled, well washed potatoes, the quartered onion, the parsley, the coriander and the salt.

3 | Put the pot on to boil and when the potatoes are almost done, add the parrotfish so that all the ingredients come to the boil together.

4 | When done, withdraw the pot from the heat and place the fish on a tray in order to remove its scales. Boil the potatoes and arrange on another tray.

5 | "Vieja Sancochada" is eaten dressed with a little oil and vinegar.

TIP The stock left over after making this dish can be used to scald the toasted flour mash together with a squashed potato. Alternatively, it may be employed in consommés or soups.

OBSERVATION A mojo verde green sauce can be made to accompany the subtle taste of this highly-esteemed Canary Island fish.

Photograph: Chopped fish platter ➤

elaborate
Fish in onions
(Encebollado de pescado)

➤ **1 kg (2¹ᐟ⁴ lb) red grouper or fish taken from fish and potato stew**
6 cloves garlic
1 green pepper
1/2 cup olive oil
5 sprigs parsley, crushed in a mortar
4 medium-sized onions
1 teaspoon oregano

1 | Leave the fish to soak the day before it is to be cooked, taking care to change the water as many times as necessary. The following morning, remove the scales from the fish and wash well under the tap with abundant cold water.

2 | Pour sufficient water into a pot and bring the fish to the boil. After a while, prod the fish with a fork to see if it is done. If tender, drain, skin and cut into pieces. Put the pieces of red grouper to one side in an ovenproof dish.

3 | Pour the oil into a frying pan. Chop up two cloves of garlic, finely slice the onion into rings and cut the pepper into strips. Fry until golden brown.

When done, sprinkle over the fish.

4 | Meanwhile, crush the remaining cloves of garlic in a mortar with the chopped parsley and oregano. Spread out over the fish and put the ovenproof dish on the heat.

5 | Leave to cook for 5 minutes. Remove from the heat and lay the fish out on a long platter decorated with wrinkled jacket potatoes.

OBSERVATION If you choose to use the salted fish left over from the fish and potato stew or "sancocho", make sure the ingredients of this recipe are adjusted accordingly.

elaborate
Fish in pickling brine
(Pescado en escabeche)

➤ **1 x 2 kg (4¹ᐟ² lb) fresh fish (red sea bream or porgy)**
hard bread, sliced
1 bulb garlic, peeled
1 tablespoon paprika
1 tablespoon oregano
2 sprigs thyme
1/4 l (9 fl oz) olive oil

1/2 kg (1 lb) small onions
1/2 sachet cumin seeds
1 bay leaf | salt
1/2 small cup water
1 small cup vinegar

1 | Remove the scales of the fish, clean well and cut into thick slices. Salt and leave in the fresh air.

2 | Once the fish has been aired, wash it with cold water and fry until golden brown. Place in an earthenware dish and set aside.

3 | Lightly fry the garlic and the slices of bread on a medium heat until golden brown, using the remaining oil that was not used to fry the fish. Take the pan off the heat and pour the contents into a mortar. Crush together with the cumin seeds and the salt.

4 | Pour this mixture into the oil in which the fish was fried and add the vinegar, thyme, paprika, bay leaf, oregano and water. Mix in well and fry for a few moments, stirring well. Later, sprinkle the fish with this seasoning. Boil for a while and then remove from the heat.

5 | Heat some oil in a pan and fry the onions until golden brown. Use them to decorate the fish. Serve cold accompanied by boiled and buttered potatoes.

Photograph: **Fish in pickling brine** ➤

Meats and garnishes

refined

Kid goat with dressing

(Cabrito (baifo) en aliño)

➤ 2 kg (4¹ᐟ² lb) kid goat (under 20 days old) |
  1 cup olive oil | 2 bulbs garlic, peeled and
  crushed | 1 cup vinegar | 1 tablespoon
  oregano, crushed | 1 red pepper, seeded |
  2 bay leaves | 1 glass white wine | 1 bunch
  thyme | 1 tablespoon cooking salt, crushed

1 | Cut the kid goat into pieces and put on one side in
a pan.

2 | Meanwhile, using a mortar and pestle, mix the
garlic, the pepper, the oregano, a little salt, the thyme,
the oil, the vinegar, the bay leaf and the white wine.

3 | Pour this dressing over the kid goat and leave it to
marinate for 24 hours.

4 | Subsequently remove the pieces of meat and fry in
a pan. At the same time, bring the dressing to the boil
and, whilst still very hot, pour over the meat.

5 | When it is done, serve the kid goat steaming hot
accompanied by a garnish of boiled and buttered or
wrinkled jacket potatoes.

easy

Traditional wrinkled jacket potatoes

(Papas arrugadas tradicionales)

➤ 2 kg (4¹ᐟ² lb) Tenerife "black" potatoes |
  1 cup salt | water, as required

1 | For this recipe, preferably buy small-sized
potatoes. Wash thoroughly. Leave in their jackets and
place in a suitable pot.

2 | Add about 2 or 3 inches of water and salt to taste.
Put on a high flame and bring the potatoes to the
boil. Then, turn the heat back down again to a
medium flame, cover with a teatowel and put the lid
back on the pot.

3 | When the potatoes are done, take the pot in both
hands and tilt from side to side until the potatoes are
dry and wrinkled. Remove from the heat, cover with
the teatowel and leave to stand for a moment.

4 | In order to avoid the potatoes going cold, serve
them one by one from the pot as required. Papas
arrugadas are best eaten hot, accompanied with any
one of the Canary Island mojo sauces.

easy
Ropa vieja

➤ 1/4 kg (9 oz) meat taken from chickpea stew | 1 kg (2¼ lb) potatoes | olive oil | 2 carrots taken from chickpea stew | 1/2 kg (1 lb) chickpeas from chickpea stew | 1 medium-sized onion | 4 cloves garlic | 1 small pepper | 1/2 teaspoon paprika | thyme and bay leaves | 3 ripe tomatoes | chopped parsley | salt

1 | Dice the meat and carrots finely and put to one side with the chickpeas.

2 | Peel and wash the potatoes. Cut into small squares and put to one side. Heat the oil in a shallow pan and lightly fry the pepper, onion and two cloves of garlic, all finely chopped.

3 | Once the mixture has been lightly fried, add the paprika, the parsley and the previously skinned, seeded and chopped tomatoes. Before they go golden brown, add the thyme and a few bay leaves. Finally, put the potatoes on to fry a little.

4 | Heat some oil in a pan and fry the two remaining cloves of garlic until golden brown. Add the chickpeas and when these too turn golden brown, transfer to the pan containing the rest of the ingredients.

5 | Fry the meat in a separate pan. Salt to taste and accompany with the carrots. When done, mix in with the other ingredients, leave on the heat for a few moments and then remove to serve.

elaborate
Gran Canaria-style rice
(Arroz a lo grancanario)

➤ 125 g (4½ oz) winkles | 1 red pepper, cut into strips | 125 g (4½ oz) beef, cut into pieces | 250 g (9 oz) rabbit, cut into pieces | 125 g (4½ oz) partridge | 250 g (9 oz) pork, cut into pieces

100 g (4 oz) Serrano cured ham, cut into pieces

125 g (4½ oz) pigeon meat, cut into pieces | 250 g (9 oz) tomatoes, skinned and seeded | 1 l (35 fl oz) stock | 1/2 onion, chopped | 1 cup olive oil | 1/2 kg (1 lb) rice | 3 cloves garlic | 1/2 teaspoon paprika

1 bunch bay leaves and thyme | 3 sprigs parsley, chopped | 1 sachet ground stick saffron | 1 clove, ground | 125 g (4½ oz) halved green beans

1 | Put water on to heat in a pot and boil the winkles (called burgados by the Canary Islanders) for 1 hour. This makes taking out the fleshy part of these mollusks that much easier; using a pin, pull the winkle out in the opposite direction to that of the spiral on the shell. Reserve on a small china tray.

2 | Heat half of the oil in a shallow earthenware dish and lightly fry a mixture prepared using the pepper, the onion, a clove of garlic and the tomatoes.

3 | Sauté all the meat in a pan. Place in a separate earthenware dish along with the ham and the bay leaves. Once these ingredients have been lightly fried, add the stock and boil until the meat is half cooked.

4 | Using the rest of the oil in another frying pan, lightly fry the remaining two cloves of garlic, sauté the rice and transfer to the dish containing the meat, along with the green beans. Cook over a high flame at first, turning down later to add the winkles, the parsley, the clove, the saffron and the paprika.

5 | Simmer for around 12 minutes. After leaving the rice to stand for 5 minutes, serve from the dish in which it has been cooked.

Photograph: **Ropa vieja** ➤

Desserts

easy

Canary Island fruit cocktail

(Ensalada de frutas de Canarias)

➤ half tropical pineapple, preferably from El Hierro | 1 average-sized papaya | 3 bananas, peeled | 1 apple | 1 medium-sized avocado | 2 oranges | the juice of 2 lemons | 1 tablespoon sugar

1 | Peel all the fruit and wash well. Once clean, dice the fruit finely and spread out over a deep, oblong tray.

2 | Sprinkle this fruit mixture with the lemon juice, add the sugar and place in the refrigerator to cool.

3 | Serve cold on individual dessert plates.

TIP To prevent the pieces of fruit turning brown, make sure you add plenty of lemon juice to the mixture.

elaborate

La Palma almond meringues (Suspiros palmeros)

➤ 150 g (5 oz) almonds | butter | 350 g (12 oz) sugar | flour | 6 egg whites

1 | After boiling, peeling and baking the almonds, crush them.

2 | Add the sugar to the egg whites and beat gently until stiff peaks are formed.

3 | Add the crushed almonds to the meringue mixture and stir gently.

4 | Grease some baking sheets with butter and dust with flour. Divide the mixture into small portions and set out on the sheets.

5 | Bake in a preheated moderate oven until golden. Ideal served as a dessert or eaten as a snack.

refined
Almond delight
(Bienmesabe)

➤ 500 g (1 lb) almonds
1/2 l (17 fl oz) water
1 grated lemon
750 g (1 lb 11 oz) sugar
8 egg yolks | ground cinnamon

1 | First of all peel the almonds and crush using a mortar and pestle. Make a syrup by mixing the water with the sugar.

2 | Add the almonds, cinnamon and grated lemon to the syrup. Heat on a low flame, stirring all the time until the mixture thickens.

3 | Once it has thickened, remove from the heat and leave to cool. Add the previously beaten egg yolks to the mixture and heat again until it boils.

4 | Take off of the heat again and eat when cool.

OBSERVATION

In some parts of the archipelago, the natural almonds used in this recipe are replaced by peeled, toasted almonds.

NOTE

"Bienmesabe" (Sp., lit. "it tastes good to me") is one of the most typical Spanish desserts, a particular variety of which is to be found in almost all the regional cuisines. What is common to all the different versions of the recipe, however, are its ingredients, namely almonds, syrup and egg yolks.

difficult
Egg in syrup
(Huevos moles)

➤ 1 large tablespoon water
8 egg yolks
To prepare the syrup:
200 g (7 oz) sugar
1 glass water
1 slice of lemon
1/2 stick cinnamon

1 | Pour the egg yolks and the water into a stainless steel or glass bowl and immediately beat in a bain-marie until a smooth, consistent mixture is obtained.

2 | Prepare the syrup using the above-mentioned ingredients. Pour the glass of water into a deep bowl, along with the sugar, the slice of lemon and the half stick of cinnamon. Beat to just the right consistency.

3 | To know whether the syrup has reached the ideal consistency, take a bit of the mixture between you thumb and forefinger and then separate thumb from finger. The syrup is just right if the thread that is formed breaks when thumb and forefinger are between 1 and 2 cm (0,39-0,78 pulgadas) apart.

4 | Once the syrup is ready, continue beating and, bit by bit, pour it over the beaten egg yolks.

5 | Serve nice and warm in individual glass bowls.

Photograph: **Almond delight** ➤

elaborate

Fig cake
(Quesos de higos pasados)

- ➤ 1 kg (2¼ lb) overripe black figs
  250 g (9 oz) walnuts
  1/2 kg (1 lb) almonds
  150 g (5 oz) flour
  1 clove, ground

1 | Remove the ends of the figs - the stalks and the tips - and grind together with the walnuts and almonds.

2 | Sprinkle the ground clove over the figs, mix in well and encircle with a brass strip or ring which, in the manner of a mould, will give the mixture the shape of a cake.

3 | Once the mixture has been placed inside the ring, dust both sides of the cake with flour, press and leave to stand for 8 days, turning every now and again. Finally, take the cake out of the ring.

4 | Cover the entire outer layer of the cake with flour and it is ready to be eaten.

OBSERVATION

This distinguished Canary Island recipe has always been the favourite dessert of the Islanders, who took it with them on emigrating to the New World. A feature of the traditional method used on the Canaries in preparing this cake is that of replacing the brass ring with a "pleita de palma", that is, a long pleated strip made from palm leaves, the string-like ends of which serve to pull the cake together.

easy

Cold rice pidding
(Arroz con leche)

- ➤ 1½ l (52 fl oz) milk
  100 g (4 oz) rice
  half a lemon rind
  100 g (4 oz) sugar
  a piece of stick cinnamon

1 | Clean the rice in water. Drain well and leave to soak in the cold milk for 3 hours.

2 | When the rice grains are well soaked, place in a pan over a low flame and continue to stir slowly until they thicken.

3 | Then add the rind of the half lemon, the sugar and the cinnamon. Keep stirring all the while.

4 | Keep cooking the mixture for a few minutes more, removing it from the flame when it has thickened completely.

5 | Leave the rice to cool in a high-sided bowl. Arroz con leche is a truly exquisite dessert.

OBSERVATION

Each guest serves himself, taking the desired amount of cold rice pudding.

TIP

Place the sugar in a separate sugar bowl, so that each person can use the amount he wishes.

Photograph: **Fig cake** ➤

easy

Cornmeal buns
(Bollos de millo)

- ➤ **200 g (7 oz) extrafine flour**
  300 g (11 oz) butter
  400 g (14 oz) cornmeal
  200 (7 oz) g sugar
  the juice and the grated rind of a lemon
  8 egg yolks
  one egg white

1 | Place all the ingredients in a large bowl and knead into a smooth dough.

2 | Dip your hands in flour and work the dough into the traditional shape for these buns (see photo opposite).

3 | Grease the baking sheets with oil. Preheat the oven to a medium temperature. Place the buns on the sheets and bake in the oven.

4 | When the buns are slightly toasted, remove from the oven and leave them to cool before serving.

OBSERVATION

"Maize" or "corn" (Sp. maíz) is known in the Canary Islands under the name of "millo". Originally found in America, this cereal crop soon became established on the archipelago and developed certain characteristics all of its own. Similarly, what we know today as "popcorn" (Sp. palomitas de maíz) was formerly called cochafisco by the Islanders.

for guests

Morello cherry liqueur
(Licor de guindilla)

- ➤ **10 l (350 fl oz) Cuban rum (40º)**
  3 l (105 fl oz) water
  6 kg (13 lb) ripe morello cherries from the Islands
  5 kg (11 lb) sugar
  half stick cinnamon

1 | De-stalk and wash the cherries before placing in a glass demijohn along with the rum.

2 | Dissolve the sugar in warm water and add the cinnamon.

3 | Transfer the sugared water with cinnamon to the glass container and leave to macerate for a year.

OBSERVATION

Although some choose to add black pepper or cloves to the mixture, we recommend that only the ingredients listed in this recipe be used, since the inclusion of any additional element will only serve to impair the taste of the morello cherries.

NOTE

"Licor de guindilla" is a renowned liqueur that is made using a bright red fruit called the morello cherry (Sp. guinda). The origin of this alcoholic beverage is to be traced to the town of San Bartolomé de Tirajana on the island of Gran Canaria.

elaborate

Almond biscuits

(Mazapán de las medianías)

➤ **1 kg sugar | grated rind of 2 lemons**
1 small glass anisette
1 kg (2¹ᐟ⁴ lb) almonds | 5 eggs

1 | Peel the almonds and heat in a pan with boiling water for a few minutes. Subsequently remove the almonds from the heat, drain and grind.

2 | Add 3/4 kg (1 lb 11 oz) sugar to the resulting almond paste. Grind again. Place in a bowl and add four egg yolks and an egg white.

3 | Mix these ingredients well. Pour in the anisette and add the grated lemon rind. Continue to mix.

4 | Grease a sheet of confectioner's paper with butter and, bit by bit, place the mixture in a brass ring, likewise greased with butter. Give the customary shape to the biscuits (see photo opposite) by squeezing the ring with your fist.

5 | Preheat the oven to a medium temperature and bake the biscuits, taking them out

before they go golden brown. Place the remaining 250 g (9 oz) sugar in a pan and heat with half a glass of water. When this syrup mixture attains an optimum degree of shine, sprinkle over the biscuits to lend them their characteristic lustre.

TIP

To obtain the necessary degree of shine to give lustre to the biscuits, check whether the syrup is done. To do this, submerge a little bit of the syrup in cold water. If it forms a little ball, it is ready and all that remains to be done is to beat it with a spatula or a rod until it whitens.

elaborate

El Hierro marzipan cakes

(Mazapanes herreños)

➤ **grated peel of 2 lemons**
puff pastry sheets, round
1 kg sugar, Icing sugar
1 kg almonds
ground cinnamon

1 | Heat some water in a saucepan. When it comes to the boil, add the almonds. Simmer

for a few minutes, remove from the heat and drain well.

2 | Mix the sugar in with the almonds and grind. Sprinkle the grated lemon rind over the resulting mass, which can now be used to form the marzipan cakes.

3 | Manually shape circles measuring 6 to 8 cm (3,8 pulgadas) in diameter and 1 cm (0,39 pulgadas) thick. Place each of these cakes over one of the round puff pastry sheets, which should be the same diameter and half as thick, joining the two together with your fingers.

4 | Transfer the marzipan cakes to an ovenproof dish and sprinkle with ground cinnamon and icing sugar. Bake in a preheated moderate oven and leave until golden. They are now ready to serve.

OBSERVATION

The basic difference between this recipe and those used to prepare other marzipans lies in the greater simplicity and subtlety of the former. Other recipes are limited to a single format and their ingredients endow the marzipan with a stronger taste and increased consistency, as is the case for example when aniseed or eggs are employed.

Canary Island Cheeses

Cheesemaking on the Canary Islands is an industry of a markedly domestic and rural nature. The explanation for this is to be found both in the perdurance of the shepherding activities that prevailed in the Guanche culture and in the fact that the replacement of the natural caves that formerly served as a shelter for the livestock by more up-to-date stabling methods has not prospered as much as might have been expected. Such a state of affairs, however, far from being a disadvantage, has endowed the local cheesemaking processes with the meticulousness characteristic of traditional handicrafts, which, combined with the sheer quality of Canary Island milk, has resulted in the production of cheeses that are matured to precisely the right degree and which thereby obtain their typical aroma and flavour.

Cheesemaking is a painstaking process whose success depends on great attention to detail, a certain amount of "savoir faire" that is handed down from generation to generation, and the acquisition of the knowledge needed to blend different types of milk in such a way that the cheeses receive the required quantity of casein and the appropriate proportion of.

Thus, by means of the curdling process the milk is coagulated using rennet (the liquid extracted from the fourth stomach of certain ruminants) or even certain plant species that allow the cheesemaker to determine the exact hardness of the curds. The purpose of the pressing of the curds is to remove any residual liquid or whey that may remain in the cheese. This is done by using either a metal ring or a pleita made from palm leaves and featuring string-like ends that can be tightened to apply pressure to the cheese. Subsequently, the cheese undergoes salting, a process which, apart from ensuring preservation, lends the cheese an enhanced flavour and guarantees the total absorption of the whey.

Finally, those cheeses intended to be cured are left to mature in special rooms. The action of certain microorganisms brings about the fermentation of the casein, which endows the cured cheeses with the properties that set them apart from other varieties.

Each cheese is a highly singular product featuring a complex combination of flavours, aromas and textures which are indicative of its origin.

Queso de Flor

Originating from the island of Gran Canaria, this cheese is made using a mixture of three parts cow's milk and one part sheep's milk and is curdled with the flower of the Cynara scolimus cardoon. Featuring a firm composition, queso de flor has a pale yellow, creamy appearance. It is smooth and buttery to the taste.

Queso palmero

Produced using goat's and sheep's milk, this cheese from La Palma has a fine appearance and a smooth texture that is a delight to savour.

Queso lanzaroteño

This cheese is made on Fuerteventura using a mixture of sheep's milk and goat's milk. It is preserved by coating its white skin in either paprika and oil or toasted flour. It has a slightly spicy flavour, one which serves to enhance its intense aroma and creaminess.

Queso majorero

This cheese is made on Fuerteventura using a mixture of sheep's milk and goat's milk. It is preserved by coating its white skin in either paprika and oil or toasted flour. It has a slightly spicy flavour, one which serves to enhance its intense aroma and creaminess.

Queso tinerfeño

Produced on Tenerife, this soft, white, slightly holed cheese features all three types of milk in equal proportions. It has an exquisite taste.

Queso de Gomera

This cheese from La Gomera is made using goat's milk and a smaller proportion of sheep's milk. A firm cheese to cut, when cured it affords a greasy appearance and has a greyish-yellowy skin. Queso de Gomera features a slightly spicy, intense flavour.

Editorial management:
Raquel López Varela
Editorial coordination:
Ángeles Llamazares Álvarez
Lay out:
Carmen García Rodríguez
Cover design:
Francisco Morais
Texts:
Eugenio O. Álvarez Á.
Translation:
EURO: TEXT, S.L. (Valladolid)
Photographs:
TRECE por DIECIOCHO;
excepto: Oliviero Daidola
(pág. 8), Paolo Tiengo (pág. 4, 5,
6, 7, 9, 11, 13), Francisco Rivero
García, (pág. 21, 27, 29, 43, 45,
47, 53, 57 y 59).

© EDITORIAL EVEREST, S. A.
Carretera León-La Coruña,
km 5 - LEÓN
ISBN: 84-241-1778-8
Legal deposit: LE: 237-2006
Printed in Spain - Impreso en España

EDITORIAL EVERGRÁFICAS, S. L.
Carretera León-La Coruña, km 5
LEÓN (ESPAÑA)

www.everest.es
Atención al cliente: 902 123 400

ABREVIATURAS:

cs = cucharada sopera
ct = cucharadita de té
fl oz = onza fluida
g = gramo
h = hora
kcal = kilocalorías
kg = kilogramo
l = litro
lb = libra
min = minuto
ml = mililitros
oz = onza

GLOSARIO DE TÉRMINOS

TABLAS DE EQUIVALENCIAS Y CONVERSIONES

España	Latinoamérica	En inglés
Albaricoque	Durazno, damasco	Apricot
Alubia blanca	Judía blanca, haba blanca	Beans
Beicon	Tocino de puerco, panceta, tocineta	Bacon
Cacahuete	Cacahuate, maní	Peanut
Calabacín	Calabacita, calabaza, zapallito	Zucchini
Callo, morro	Mondongo	Tripe
Cochinillo	Lechón, cochinita, cerdito	Piglet
Creps	Crepas, panqueque, arepas	Crêpe
Dulce, membrillo	Ate, dulce de cereza	Quince
Entremés	Botana, copetín, entremeses	Hors d'oeuvre
Especias diversas	Recaudo	Spice
Filete	Escalopa, bife, biftec	Steak
Fresa	Frutilla	Strawberry
Gamba	Camarón	Schrimp
Guisante	Chícharo, arveja, habichuelas	Pea
Helado	Nieve, mantecado	Ice-cream
Judía verde	Ejote, chaucha	String bean
Maíz	Elote, choclo	Corn
Melocotón	Durazno	Peach
Nata	Crema de leche, crema doble, natilla	Cream
Patata	Papa	Potato
Pavo	Guajolote	Turkey
Pimiento verde	Ají	Pepper
Plátano	Plátano macho, banana, guineo	Banana
Salpicón	Ceviche, ceviche criollo	
Salsa	Aliño, mole	Sauce
Sésamo	Ajonjolí	Sesame
Setas	Hongos, mushrooms	Mushrooms
Tomate rojo	Jitomate, tomate	Tomato
Tortilla	Torta, omelette, omellete	Omelet
Zumo	Jugo, néctar	Juice

PESO

Sistema métrico	Sistema anglosajón
30 g	1 onza (oz)
110 g	4 oz (1/4 lb)
225 g	8 oz (1/2 lb)
340 g	12 oz (3/4 lb)
450 g	16 oz (1 lb)
1 kg	$2^{1/4}$ lb
1,8 kg	4 lb

CAPACIDAD (líquidos)

ml	fl oz (onzas fluidas)
30 ml	1 fl oz
100 ml	$3^{1/2}$ fl oz
150 ml	5 fl oz
200 ml	7 fl oz
500 ml	17 fl oz
1 l	35 fl oz

LONGITUD

pulgadas	equivalente métrico
1 pulgada	2,54 cm
5 pulgadas	12,70 cm
10 pulgadas	25,40 cm
15 pulgadas	38,10 cm
20 pulgadas	50,80 cm

TEMPERATURAS (Horno)

°C	°F	Gas
70	150	1/4
100	200	1/2
150	300	2
200	400	6
220	425	7
250	500	9